Ten Key People from the Bible

by Jeanette B. Strandjord

Bible Basics for Adults

Augsburg Fortress, Minneapolis

Contents

BIBLE BASICS FOR ADULTS
Ten Key People from the Bible Learner Book
This learner book has a corresponding leader guide.

Editors: Mary Nasby Lohre and Alyn Beckman
Designer: Craig P. Claeys
Illustrators: Julie Delton, Mari Goering, and Parrot Graphics/Patti Isaacs
Photographer: Richard T. Nowitz

Unless otherwise noted, scripture quotations are from New Revised Standard Version Bible, copyright 1989 Division of Christian Education of the National Council of the Churches of Christ in the United States of America. Used by permission.

ISBN 0-8066-2323-3

Manufactured in U.S.A.
1 2 3 4 5 6 7 8 9 0 1 2 3 4 5 6 7 8 9

❶ God Keeps Promises

God keeps promises to the chosen people in spite of their fears and doubts.

Genesis 18:1-15 Abraham and the Promise

Just Imagine!

TRY TO PUT YOURSELF in the shoes of Abraham and Sarah that hot afternoon so long ago. God has promised you that your descendants will be many, but instead you find yourself childless and too old to bear children. Descendants seem impossible, and the land of Canaan God led you into has not been as wonderful as you had hoped it would be. Instead of abundance, you have experienced famine.

Besides this, you must also wrestle with your own failures. Tired of waiting for a child, you plot together for Abraham to conceive a child with the slave Hagar. A son, Ishmael, is born. But God did not approve of your plan, and so you continue to wait.

One day as you are camped by the side of the road, three visitors suddenly appear. As Abraham, you jump up to offer them generous hospitality as God has commanded. As Sarah, you hurry to prepare the cakes. It is improper for you to be seen, so you listen behind the tent door and hear some unbelievable news. You hear you will have a baby in your old age! You laugh and are caught. You deny the laughing, but the visitors are not fooled. Despite your laughter, the promise holds. The visitors leave, and you are left waiting. In imagining, we begin to learn important things about Abraham, Sarah, God, and God's people.

> **The name *Abraham*** means "ancestor of a multitude."

Sarah and Abraham are described as "advanced in age" (verse 11)—a short phrase that tells us that the promise of a son has been a long time in coming. Sarah and Abraham, as God's people, are called to be a patient, waiting people. Two ways to wait are contrasted in this passage. Abraham waits patiently. He is the model of the hospitality demanded by God. His invitation opens the way for the visitors' good news. When the news is announced, he does not laugh as he did earlier (see Genesis 17:17). Instead, he quietly trusts. But Sarah does laugh, and fear and denial follow. Sarah represents that part of God's people, then and now, that is worn down by waiting against impossible odds. After all, it is difficult to trust that God can deliver in such circumstances.

> **Isaac is the name** of the promised son. *Isaac* means "he laughs."

God is also a major player in this story. The first two words in this passage, "The LORD" (18:1), tell us it is God who is present in these three visitors. Abraham's greeting of "My lord" (verse 3) does not mean he recognizes God. It is merely a polite address. God's disguise is not to be seen as a trick, but as a bit of a test. God commanded hospitality to travelers and strangers. Abraham is faithful and gives it. God proves to be a God of surprises who calls for obedience.

God also proves to be faithful in spite of human doubt. Sarah laughs, and Abraham has laughed at the same news earlier. God meets such disbelief with firm faithfulness. This is seen most clearly in the visitor's question, "Is anything too wonderful for the LORD?" (verse 14). Despite impossible odds and frail human faith, God will give Abraham and Sarah a baby boy. This son will show that there is nothing too difficult or wonderful for God to do.

> **The Lord appeared** to Abraham at the "oaks of Mamre." It was here that a son was promised to Abraham and Sarah.

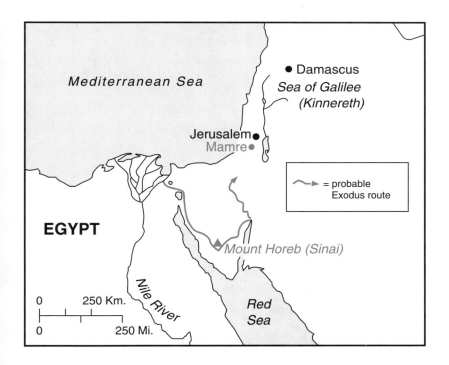

Exodus 3:1-15 Moses and the Burning Bush

Questions! Questions!

IN THIS TEXT, God's people (the Hebrews) are in slavery in Egypt. After years of peace a new pharaoh persecutes them (Exodus 1:8 and following). God knows the misery and suffering of the Hebrews and intends to rescue them. But how will God go up against Egypt with its sophisticated army and great resources of wealth?

Enter Moses. We find him watching sheep in the wilderness near Mount Horeb. (*Horeb* means "wasteland.") He has shown compassion for others in the past. He once killed an Egyptian in defense of a Hebrew slave (Exodus 2:ll and following). But now he has run away and leads a quiet life.

Enter the burning bush. God wants to get Moses' attention. A flame burns within a bush, but the bush does not burn up. God's plan works, and Moses is curious. Fire is an important symbol of God's power, presence, and promise in the Bible. Later in the story of

God's people, God appears in a pillar of fire (Exodus 13:2l) and gifts them with the Spirit through "tongues of fire" (see Acts 2:3).

The name *Moses* means "drawn out" and refers to him being drawn out of the Nile by the pharaoh's daughter (Exodus 2).

Moses doesn't become afraid until God speaks his name. Then he realizes he is meeting God in this burning bush, and he knows seeing God can mean death (Exodus 33:20). Moses hides, but a very open and revealing conversation with God follows.

Early in the conversation God tells Moses, "I am the God of your father" (3:6). God has a history with Moses and his people,

Mount Horeb, the mountain of God, is also known as Mount Sinai.

and that history includes the covenant with Abraham (see Genesis 12 and 15). God will be faithful to this and deliver the Hebrews from their misery and oppression.

God goes even further in this conversation and promises Moses a sign. The sign will be that once the Hebrews are rescued, they will all return to this very place and worship God. Later this proves to be true as they come to Mount Sinai after the Exodus (Exodus 19).

God reveals God's name as additional information and assurance for Moses. The name is "I AM WHO I AM" (verse 14). By revealing this name, God is tied even more closely with Moses and his people. What God is saying through this particular name is "I am really here, ready to help as I have always been."

BIBLICAL LIFE LINES

Creation	**Genesis 1:1—2:4a**
The Fall	**Genesis 3:1-24**
The Flood	**Genesis 6:11-22; 9:8-17**
Call of Abraham	**Genesis 12:1-3**
2100 B.C.	Abraham's covenant
Abraham and Sarah	**Genesis 18:1-15**
1526 B.C.	Moses' birth
Moses	**Exodus 3:1-15**
1275–1235 B.C.	Exodus

See the time line on pages 24-25.

This name is no mere statement that God exists. Rather, it is a revealed name for God that Moses can share with the people. It says that God is on the move to help here and now.

This story also tells us much about Moses. Throughout the narrative, Moses shows a very normal human response to God's words. Twice he objects and tries to dodge the call to be God's messenger.

> **Moses objects** to God's call many times in Exodus (3:6, 11, 13; 4:1, 10, 13; 5:22-23; 6:12, 30). God meets those objections with encouragement for Moses.

He pleads unworthiness (verse 11) and ignorance (verse 13). Later, he worries whether or not he will be believed and whether his speech impediment will be an insurmountable problem (Exodus 4). Moses is not sure of himself or God, and he has no trouble telling God about it. He does recognize God's holiness, but this doesn't prevent honest questioning and even disagreement. In fact, this ongoing conversation leads Moses to a greater understanding of and close relationship with God.

It is a faithful God who enlists Moses to help free God's people. Doubts and all, Moses goes forward, equipped with the promise that God is his strength and constant companion.

> **Zipporah is** Moses' wife, and Gershom is his son.

Focus the Stories

God's Surprises

Both Bible passages reveal God as a God of surprises. Why do you think God surprises Abraham and Sarah through the three visitors or Moses through the burning bush? Is there something about us human beings that makes this necessary? Has God ever surprised you through someone or some event?

What Do You Think?

God and Moses have a long, productive conversation, including questions and objections. Brainstorm a list of questions your group might have asked God if you had been Moses. Or divide the group in two and have one half ask questions and the other try to answer them from God's point of view. You may also write down your own faith questions and turn these in, no names attached. Discuss them. If questions arise that no one can answer, try to find answers for them to share at the next session.

Open Doors

There is an old saying "When one door closes, God opens another." Does this apply to our Bible readings? If so, how? Can you think of an instance when it might apply to your life or the life of someone you know?

Update

If the story of Moses' call took place today, what setting and characters would you use to tell it?

A Cloud of Witnesses

We are surrounded in the Bible and in our daily lives with many faithful witnesses to the love and faithfulness of God. These people nurture our faith. How would you complete these sentences?

• If I could adopt one characteristic of **Moses** it would be _____ because _____.

• If I could adopt one characteristic of **Abraham** or **Sarah** it would be _____ because _____.

Closing

O God, our help in ages past,
Our hope for years to come,
Our shelter from the stormy blast,
And our eternal home.

② God's Power at Work

God works through responsible and courageous people to accomplish God's plan of salvation.

Ruth 1:1-18 Ruth the Foreigner

A Courageous Choice

MEET RUTH, A WOMAN OF THE OLD TESTAMENT who was given the rare compliment of being more valuable than seven sons (Ruth 4:15). In a time when blessing and security came for a family through its sons, this was a great compliment indeed! What is special about Ruth is her courage and loyalty.

> **The name *Ruth* means** "beloved." *Chilion* and *Mahlon* (the names of Naomi's sons) mean "sickly."

At first glance we see Ruth as a powerless woman. Her husband is dead, and she has no property and very few rights. It appears that her only hope is to return to Moab, the home of her origin, and find a husband. Naomi has no other sons for Ruth to marry (verse 11), and so the levirite marriage command, which directs a man to marry his brother's widow (Deuteronomy 25:5-10), cannot be fulfilled. (Genesis 38 tells the story of Judah and Tamar, an example of how this marriage command worked.)

> **Moab is east** of the Dead Sea.

When Ruth's mother-in-law, Naomi, gives her the opportunity to return to Moab, she refuses. Instead Ruth pledges,

"Your people shall be my people, and your God my God" (verse 16). For Ruth to leave her own land was to cut herself off from her people and her gods and to leave everything behind. This was no small matter.

When she heads for Bethlehem, Ruth goes from very little security to even less. Ruth is a foreigner, but one who turns to Naomi's God. When she says that

> Bethlehem is five miles south of Jerusalem.

Naomi's God is her God, she uses the familiar Hebrew name *Yahweh*. This is a sign of her genuine faith. Immediately after this she pledges total commitment by saying, "Where you die, I will die"

> The name *Naomi* means "my pleasure."

(verse 17). Even if Naomi died, Ruth is determined to remain in her new homeland with her new God until the end of her life.

Such courage and loyalty are powerful tools in the hands of God. Once Ruth and Naomi reach Bethlehem (Ruth 2), God goes to work to give them a just future. Ruth's courage and loyal obedience to Naomi lead her to Naomi's kinsman Boaz. After a short time and much maneuvering by Naomi (Ruth 3), Boaz fulfills his obligation to Naomi by marrying Ruth. This marriage gives Ruth and Naomi security, and it produces a child, Obed. Obed is to be the grandfather of King David. It is through David that God will deliver the promised savior for God's people.

A key word that appears often in Ruth's story is *kinsman*. Naomi laments that in Moab there is none for her (verses 11-13). Boaz is referred to as one (Ruth 2:l; 3:2, 12, 13). To act the part of a kinsman is to

LINEAGE OF JESUS (Matthew 1:1-17)

Abraham
Isaac
Jacob
Judah
Perez (by Tamar)
Hezron
Aram
Aminadab
Nahshon
Salmon
Boaz
Obed (by Ruth)
Jesse
David
Solomon (by Bathsheba)
Rehoboam
Abijah
Asa
Jehoshaphat
Joram
Uzziah
Jotham
Ahaz
Hezekiah
Manasseh
Amos
Josiah
Jechoniah
Salathiel
Zerubbabel
Abiud
Eliakim
Azor
Zadok
Achim
Eliud
Eleazar
Matthan
Jacob
Joseph (husband of Mary)
Jesus Christ

redeem or take responsibility for someone else. This is exactly what Boaz does for Ruth and Naomi. He honors the duty God has given him to marry Ruth. In this story we have Ruth who, through courage and loyalty, places herself in God's land and care, and Boaz who, through loyalty and obedience, does what is right in God's sight. Naomi's loyalty in returning to her homeland and her courage in bringing together Ruth and Boaz are vital too. God works through these faithful people to bring justice to Ruth and Naomi and to produce a baby who will be an important part of God's long-term plan of salvation.

2 Samuel 7:1-29 David's Covenant with God

Bold Humility

DAVID'S LIFE IS SOMETHING of a "rags to riches" story. Formerly a young, handsome, humble shepherd boy (1 Samuel 16:1-13), David first becomes a national military hero and then the King of Israel. He cuts a dashing figure as king, too, for he is confident, ambitious, and bold. His boldness shows up in his relationship with others and in his relationship with the Lord.

In verses 18-29 we find David the king praying, kneeling humbly before God. In the first part of his prayer David humbly thanks the Lord for all that he has received (verses 18-21). It is the Lord, not David, who has "wrought all this greatness" (verse 21). David is well aware that it is only by the power and grace of God that a shepherd boy came to triumph over his enemies and become king (verses 8-9). David praises God's unequaled greatness and clearly recognizes that only God is responsible for Israel's victory (verses 22-24).

> **"Sat before the Lord"** means to kneel before God.

Humility and praise are followed by demands (verses 25-29). "And now," says David in a demanding tone (verse 25). This introductory phrase implies that David is saying, "*Therefore* I expect you to keep your part of the bargain." Nowhere does God scold David for using such a tone. It seems they understand each other, and God has every intention of keeping the promise, or covenant, made to David.

God's promise to build David a "house" (verse 11) is the heart of the covenant. The "house" is understood to mean a dynasty, not a building. It will last forever. God's steadfast love will never be taken from David or his descendants as it was taken from the previous king, Saul (verse 16). God will not hesitate to punish iniquity or sin,

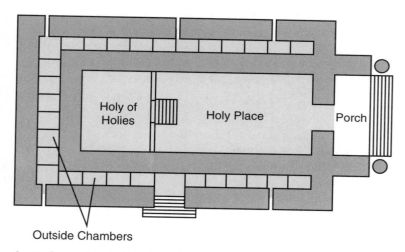

Outside Chambers

A temple was later built in Jerusalem by David's son Solomon (1 Kings 5–6).

and we see that happen after David admits his unfaithfulness to God involving Bathsheba (2 Samuel 12:13-14). But even then, God's promise will not end. The line of David is part of God's long-term plan of salvation.

One can imagine how confident this made David feel, not to mention the effect it had on the entire nation of Israel. Israel could be a community of hope even in times of uncertainty and defeat. Indeed, this unconditional promise reached far into the future, and Christians saw it fulfilled in Jesus Christ (Luke 2:4).

> **The name *David*** means "commander" or "hero."

The immediate setting into which God's incredible promise, or covenant, comes is important. The prophet Nathan speaks God's promise when David is planning to build a house or temple for

God (verse 5). God will not have it and refuses to issue a building permit. There is a warning to David and all Israel implied in the words spoken through Nathan. God will not be limited or confined to any human-made building (verses 6-7). God will always be a God freely on the move. God, not David, will be the builder. King David and Israel are reminded of who is the provider. Success can

and will tempt them to forget that truth (2 Samuel 12:1-25; 1 Kings 11:1-13). Bold faith is called for, but it can become dangerous when the people forget the one who is the true builder.

Focus the Stories

God Still at Work

Who are some modern counterparts of the faithful Ruth, Naomi, and Boaz? Where are Christians called to be both courageous and obedient to God these days? How could this lead to good?

Kin to All

In a world where we are increasingly interconnected through communication, travel, economics, and environmental concerns, we could say, "Everyone is my neighbor or kin." Do you agree? What responsibilities do we have to our global neighbors? Are there limits to them?

Redeem It

Make a coupon offering your time, energy, or talent to help a member of your family or a close friend. It could read: "Redeem this coupon for _____." Fill in something appropriate for that person. *(For instance, bake his or her favorite dessert, wash his or her car, or offer to take a long walk together.)* Share that coupon today.

Remember It

Make your own time line of God's gracious acts in your life or the history of your family. David remembered these acts and was able to recount them. Your list might include your baptism, a favorite teacher, a new friend, or rescue from sickness or harm.

A Cloud of Witnesses

We are surrounded in the Bible and in our daily lives with many faithful witnesses to the love and faithfulness of God. These people nurture our faith. How would you complete these sentences?

- If I could adopt one characteristic of **Ruth** it would be _____ because _____.
- If I could adopt one characteristic of **David** it would be _____ because _____.

Closing

Now let us be united, and let our song be heard.
Now let us be a vessel for God's redeeming Word.
We all are one in mission; we all are one in call,
our varied gifts united by Christ, the Lord of all.

③ Judges and Prophets

God blesses men and women with good judgment and leadership skills to deliver God's people.

Judges 4:1-24 Deborah the Judge

Follow the Leader

BARAK, THE ISRAELITE GENERAL, led thousands of troops into fierce battle (verses 14-16). The name *Barak* means "lightning," and this text gives the impression that he feared very little in life. It is difficult to imagine him refusing to go into battle without the company of the woman Deborah, but this is what happens. Barak says to Deborah before the great battle with General Sisera (verse 8), "If you will go with me, I will go; but if you will not go with me, I will not go." Deborah goes, and she even gives the order to charge (verse 14)! This woman, both judge and prophet, is someone special in the history of Israel.

> The name *Sisera* means "leader."

Deborah is respected by Barak because of her calling as a judge in Israel. The word *judge* is best translated as "deliverer" or "savior." A judge was a person of great moral authority and spiritual insight, one called by God to arbitrate personal disputes and give advice to all who came to her or him. Deborah spent much of her time hearing cases and settling disputes over property and rights among the people (verses 4-5). When there was an external threat to God's

people, the judge lead the people into battle. The people of Israel, including mighty warriors, believed the judge was gifted by God with spiritual insight, and so they followed.

Judges usually appeared in Israel's history during times of oppression and trouble. As Israel settled into the new land of Canaan, there were many disputes with neighboring foreign tribes. Deborah judged at a time when King Jabin oppressed God's people (verse 2), sometime around 1150 B.C. The reason for this oppression was Israel's own sin (verse 1). Most often in the book of Judges, that sin was worshiping local fertility gods. Jabin's harshness was God's judgment on this sin. Under this severe judgment of 20 years, Israel repented (verse 3), and as a result, God sent Deborah to lead and deliver them.

JUDGES	1200–1050 B.C.
We know the most about these six judges in Israel's history:	
Othniel	**Judges 3:7-11**
Ehud	**Judges 3:12-30**
Deborah	**Judges 4–5**
Gideon	**Judges 6:1—8:32**
Jephthah	**Judges 10:6—12:7**
Samson	**Judges 13–16**

This pattern runs throughout Judges and much of the Old Testament. Israel sins *(chases after false gods)*, God sends judgment *(foreign invasion)*, Israel repents *(turns to God for help)*, and God delivers *(raises up a judge or leader)*. The pattern is used to explain a great deal of Israel's history. God takes a very active role in the lives of God's people, working through many people, events, and even the weather!

In the great battle, Sisera and his chariots have to cross the brook Wadi Kishon (verse 13). Deborah says to Barak, "The LORD is indeed going out before you" (verse 14). She implies that in some visible way God is present, as God has always been—often through thunder clouds or a storm. This certainly seems to be the case here. The stream floods, and Sisera's mighty chariots bog down in the mud (Judges 5:21). Mired in the muck, the Canaanites panic and are defeated. God delivers Israel through Deborah's leadership, Barak's allegiance, and even the natural elements.

Hazor is nine miles north of the Sea of Galilee. Mount Tabor is 1,850 feet high.

Jeremiah 1:4-19 Jeremiah's Call

Strong Youth, Stubborn Ground

J EREMIAH IS JUST A BOY OF 18 YEARS at the time of this Bible story. His country is in upheaval. He has a vision and in it discovers a call to be a prophet to the nations (verse 5). He is to carry God's word, a strong word of judgment (verse 10). Jeremiah's career as a prophet lasts about 40 years. It involves personal and national agony (Jeremiah 4–6), brief moments of hope (Jeremiah 7:1-7), and finally complete disaster (Jeremiah 39). Through all of it, God is at work to rescue the chosen people (Jeremiah 31:31-34).

What does it mean to be a prophet? The call of Jeremiah (verses 5-10) gives us a basic answer. A prophet is someone appointed by God (verse 5) to speak God's word (verse 7). Literally, a prophet is to be God's own mouthpiece (verse 9). God places the divine word directly into Jeremiah's mouth in order to speak to a specific people in a specific situation (verses 14-15). In Jeremiah's case, these words are to be words of judgment for God's people in Judah.

OLD TESTAMENT PROPHETS		
Isaiah	755 B.C.	(Judah)
Jeremiah	626 B.C.	(Judah)
Ezekiel	592 B.C.	(Judah)
Hosea	785 B.C.	(Israel)
Joel	800 B.C.	(Judah)
Amos	787 B.C.	(Israel)
Obadiah	887 B.C.	(Judah)
Jonah	862 B.C.	(Ninevah)
Micah	750 B.C.	(Judah)
Nahum	713 B.C.	(Judah)
Habakkuk	626 B.C.	(Judah)
Zephaniah	630 B.C.	(Judah)
Haggai	520 B.C.	
Zechariah	520 B.C.	
Malachi	397 B.C.	

(Continued on page 27)

HOW THE BIBLE IS ORGANIZED

The Bible is divided into two "testaments." The Old Testament, which was originally written in Hebrew, contains four major sections that include 39 individual books. The New Testament, which was originally written in Greek, is divided into three sections that include 27 books.

THE OLD TESTAMENT

The Pentateuch
Genesis
Exodus
Leviticus
Numbers
Deuteronomy

History
Joshua
Judges
Ruth
1 and 2 Samuel
1 and 2 Kings
1 and 2 Chronicles
Ezra
Nehemiah
Esther

Wisdom
Job
Psalms
Proverbs

Ecclesiastes
Song of Solomon

Prophets
Isaiah
Jeremiah
Lamentations
Ezekiel
Daniel
Hosea
Joel
Amos
Obadiah
Jonah
Micah
Nahum
Habakkuk
Zephaniah
Haggai
Zechariah
Malachi

THE NEW TESTAMENT

The Gospels
Matthew
Mark
Luke
John

History
Acts of the Apostles

The Letters
Romans
1 and 2 Corinthians
Galatians
Ephesians

Philippians
Colossians
1 and 2 Thessalonians
1 and 2 Timothy
Titus
Philemon
Hebrews
James
1 and 2 Peter
1, 2, and 3 John
Jude
Revelation

Adapted from *A Beginner's Guide to Reading the Bible* by Craig R. Koester, copyright © 1991 Augsburg Fortress.

BIBLE TIME LINE

Date	Bible Story/Message	Text
	Creation	Genesis 1:1 — 2:4a
	The Fall	Genesis 3:1-24
	The Flood	Gen. 6:11-22; 9:8-17
	Call of Abraham	Genesis 12:1-3
	Abraham and Sarah	Genesis 18:1-15
	Moses	Exodus 3:1-15
1275-1235 B.C.	Exodus and Wilderness Wandering	
	Wilderness Wandering	Exodus 16:1-12
	The Ten Commandments	Exodus 20:1-17
	The Shema	Deuteronomy 6:4-9
1200-1050 B.C.	Judges	
	Deborah and Barak	Judges 4:1-24
	Ruth and Naomi	Ruth 1:1-18
1050-922 B.C.	United Monarchy	
	David	2 Samuel 7:1-29
	The Divine Shepherd	Psalm 23:1-6
	Thanks for Healing	Psalm 30:4-5
922-721 B.C.	Divided Monarchy	
	Micah	Micah 6:8
	Jeremiah	Jeremiah 1:4-19
	The Fiery Furnace	Daniel 3:1-30
	Fall of Northern Kingdom	2 Kings 17:5-23
586-538 B.C.	Judah in Exile	
538-333 B.C.	Persian Period	
333-165 B.C.	Hellenistic Period	
165-63 B.C.	Maccabean Period	
63 B.C.-A.D. 637	Roman Period	
	Mary	Luke 1:26-38

Date	Bible Story/Message	Text
4 B.C.	Jesus is Born	
	Birth of Jesus	Luke 2:1-20
	Birth of Jesus	Matthew 1:1, 17-25
	Baptism of Jesus	Matthew 3:13-17
	Temptation of Jesus	Luke 4:1-13
A.D. 20	Ministry of Jesus	
	Sermon on the Mount	Matthew 7:1-12
	Healing a Paralytic	Mark 2:1-12
	The Gospel in Miniature	John 3:16
	Cleansing the Temple	Mark 11:15-19
	Mary and Martha	Luke 10:38-42
	Peter	Matthew 16:13-23
	The Lord's Supper	Matthew 26:17-30
	I Am the Way	John 14:6
	The Crucifixion	Mark 15:21-39
	The Death of Jesus	John 19:1-30
	The Road to Emmaus	Luke 24:13-35
	Jesus' Resurrection	John 20:1-18
	The Ascension of Jesus	Acts 1:6-11
	Pentecost	Acts 2:1-14, 37-42
A.D. 40	Apostles' Ministry	
	Paul	Acts 9:1-22
	Benediction	2 Thess. 2:16-17
	A New Creation	2 Cor. 5:17-21
	God's Love in Christ Jesus	Romans 8:31-39
	By Grace	Ephesians 2:8-10
	Faith	Hebrews 11:1-3
	Encouragement and Warnings	Hebrews 12:1-2
	The Alpha and Omega	Revelation 1:8

HOW TO READ THE BIBLE

Finding a Bible Reference

1. Check the Bible's table of contents if you do not know where the book is.
2. In your Bible, the chapter numbers are large numbers, usually at the beginning of paragraphs. The chapter numbers might be also printed at the top of each page.
3. The verse numbers are tiny numbers, usually printed at the beginning of sentences.

Psalm 119:105		
book of the Bible	chapter	verse

Understanding What You Read

As you read a passage of the Bible, keep in mind these three questions:

1. What does this text tell me about God?
2. What does this text tell me about the people of God?
3. What does this text tell me about myself?

Going Deeper

Other questions that might help you understand what you are reading include:

1. What type of literature is this passage? Is it a story? A historical account? Poetry? A hymn? A letter? How might that affect my understanding of the passage?
2. What is the historical situation of the writer?
3. Who is speaking in this passage?
4. Who is being addressed in this passage? How am I like or different from that person or group?
5. How does the passage relate to the surrounding text? Does the surrounding material shed any light on the passage's meaning?
6. What are the key words and phrases in the passage? Which ones do I not understand?
7. How does the passage compare to parallel passages or to texts on the same subject?
8. What in the passage puzzles, surprises, or confuses me?

Marking Your Bible

When you read the Bible, make notes to yourself about questions and insights you have as you read. The following symbols might be helpful.

   ㉓ The circled number marks an important chapter.
   ? I do not understand this.
   ♥ God's love is revealed in this passage.
   P One of God's promises is given here.
   † This is about something God has done for me.
   HS The work of the Holy Spirit is described here.
   F Faith, confidence, trust
   H Hope, perseverance, patience
   ↔ Love, relationships, social concerns
   ✍ Prayer
   ♪ Praise, joy, hymns
   ℞ Strength, comfort, healing

"Going Deeper" and "Marking Your Bible" are adapted from *Bible Reading Handbook* by Paul Schuessler, copyright © 1991 Augsburg Fortress.

(Continued from page 22)

Jeremiah's prophecy tells the people that disaster is coming from the north (verses 11-16). Jeremiah has two visions that are central to his call and prophecy.

• First, Jeremiah sees the "branch of an almond tree" (verse 11), and God promises to continue to be "watching over my word to perform it" (verse 12). The Hebrew words for "almond" and "watch" are very similar, and a play on words is intended. It is as if God is saying, "See that lookout tower up there? Well let that remind you that I will be looking out after my word and you." The message in this first vision is that God will watch and make sure that what God has spoken will happen.

• The second vision is the ominous one of a "boiling pot, tilted away from the north" (verse 13). God's people have worshiped other gods and corrupted their social and religious life, so now they will be invaded (verses 15-16). Even Jerusalem, Judah's capital, will fall. The contents of this "boiling pot" in Jeremiah's vision are about to "spill" in a southerly direction. In the future, this happens, indeed, when the Babylonians overrun Judah (chapter 39).

> **The name *Jeremiah*** means "God will elevate."

What a word to bring to your own people! At a young age Jeremiah would have to speak harsh words to kings, princes, priests, and "the people of the land" (verse 18). This last phrase is a technical term for the important land

> **The priest Pashhur** struck Jeremiah and put him in stocks (Jeremiah 20:1-2).

holders in Judah. Jeremiah will have to confront rich and powerful people.

Baruch was Jeremiah's disciple and scribe, or recorder. The name *Baruch* means "blessed."

In the image of Jeremiah, we see a youth harnessed to a plow that must till the stubborn sod of human will. It is exhausting work, but until the ground is broken nothing can grow. God's word is to be the blade of the plow, and Jeremiah must speak that word again and again. Once the ground is broken and the people repent, God will work deliverance and bring new hope to the people.

Jeremiah lived during a time when Assyria, Babylon, and Egypt struggled to control the known world. This included the Egyptian domination of Jerusalem in 609 B.C., its capture by the Chaldeans in 597 B.C., and its destruction by the Babylonians in 587. His life was framed within events that occurred during the reigns of the last Judean kings:

Manasseh	(687-642 B.C)	2 Chronicles 33:1-20
Amon	(642-640 B.C.)	2 Chronicles 33:21-24
Josiah	(640-609 B.C.)	2 Kings 21:24—23:30
Jehoahaz	(609 B.C.)	2 Kings 23:30-33
Jehoiakim	(609-598 B.C.)	2 Kings 23:34—24:6
Jehoiachin	(598-597 B.C.)	2 Kings 24:6-15
Zedekiah	(597-587 B.C.)	2 Kings 24:17-21

Focus the Stories

Where Are They Today?

Have you ever known people like Deborah or Jeremiah? Who are they? What part have they played in your life, community, or world? Is there a bit of Deborah or Jeremiah in you? When do you act as a fair and wise mediator? When are you an honest and hopeful critic?

Then and Now

What similarities do you see in the social and religious situations of our time and Jeremiah's time?

Play the Prophet

Write your own prophecy for today. Name one sin, pronounce God's judgment on it, and then call the people to acts of repentance. Close with a promise of God's deliverance. Jeremiah 7:3-7 is a good example of a prophetic speech. Use it as a guideline for writing your own. Some possible subject areas are environmental concerns *(Is pollution of air and water a sin?)*; health issues *(Is drug abuse a sin?)*; or societal issues *(Is stock market fraud a sin?)*. Take turns reading your prophecies to each other.

A Cloud of Witnesses

We are surrounded in the Bible and in our daily lives with many faithful witnesses to the love and faithfulness of God. These people nurture our faith. How would you complete these sentences?

- If I could adopt one characteristic of **Deborah** it would be _____ because _____.
- If I could adopt one characteristic of **Jeremiah** it would be _____ because _____.

Closing

Herald, sound the note of judgment,
Warning us of right and wrong,
Turning us from sin and sadness
Till once more we sing the song.
Sound the trumpet! Tell the message:
Christ, the Savior king, is come!

4 God's Powerful Presence

God's people learn to listen and trust.

Luke 1:26-38 Mary the Mother of Jesus

Humble Faith, Great Gift

ABRAHAM AND SARAH LAUGHED. Moses objected. King David demanded. *Mary trusted.* All along, God has been at work doing the impossible in order to save Israel and the world. Now in this passage, to this young, unmarried, small-town girl, God announces that she will bear the Son of God, who will save the people. Her response is one of faith and humility.

We know that something big is afoot because Gabriel, one of the most important members of God's heavenly council, is sent as God's messenger to the insignif-

> **The name *Gabriel*** means "man of God."

icant village of Nazareth (verse 26). Gabriel's visit is significant, as it has been in the past (Daniel 8:16; 9:21). The title "favored one" (verse 28) would be startling to this young girl, who is somewhere between the age of 12 and 18 years. "Favored one" means to be one who is to receive a gift. This girl has been chosen to serve God by giving birth to God's greatest gift, the Christ child. And she will be empowered by God's presence.

> **The name *Mary*** means "exalted one."

Jesus is the Greek form of the Hebrew name Joshua.

Mary will be empowered by God to carry the gift generations of Israelites have been waiting for: the Savior. Jesus, whose name means "God saves," is coming (verse 31), and Mary will be his mother. But here's the rub. Mary is engaged but not yet married. She rightly wonders, "How can this be?" (verse 34) because she has not had sexual relations with any man. Gabriel explains that the power of God (or the Holy Spirit) will "overshadow" Mary. Overshadowing is a way to describe the protecting and powerful presence of God. We see this elsewhere in the Scriptures when God is

Luke 1:31 is the fulfillment of Isaiah 7:14.

with the people in the form of a cloud to protect them (Exodus 40:34-38) and when God comes in a cloud at Jesus' transfiguration (Luke 9:34-35). God's powerful presence will rest upon Mary, and she will bear a child who will be both human and the divine Son of God.

To all of this Mary replies, "Here am I, the servant of the Lord" (verse 38). This is an incredible response of trust in the face of such impossibilities. Mary is a model of faith for us all in her willingness to trust God. She does not laugh, object, or demand. In almost direct contrast to Zechariah, who asks for a sign a few verses earlier (1:12-20), Mary believes. Humbly she says, "Let it be with me according to your word" (verse 38). This willingness to be a servant of God is to become a mark of identity for all Christians. Jesus will call all believers to a life of trust and service (Luke 9:23-27; 14:11). These believers will serve by the power of God's Spirit as they preach and heal in the early church (Acts 2:18; 4:29-30).

The child Mary is to bear will be the culmination of God's saving work. Jesus fulfills God's promise to build a house for David (verses 27, 32). He is different from all of God's other chosen servants because he is truly God's own divine Son (verse 35). What Jesus accomplishes will last forever (verse 33). He is the fulfillment of everything promised in the "law of Moses, the prophets, and the psalms" (24:44). Through the humble faith of Mary, God gives us Jesus the Christ to bring repentance, forgivness of sins, and new life to Israel and the world (24:46-49).

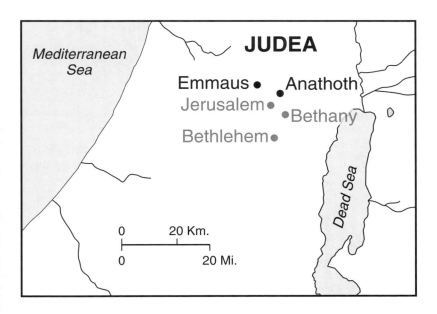

Luke 10:38-42   Mary's Visit with Jesus

Breaking the Mold

O LIVIA HAD THE NICEST ROOM in the nursing home. There was a color television, beautiful quilt, cozy robe and slippers, fresh flowers, stereo, and recliner. Still she lamented one day, "Oh, if only my children would stop sending me all this stuff and just come and see me." Frail Olivia knew what was important to her. It wasn't the "creature comforts"—it was a relationship with her children.

The importance of relationship also comes up in this story of Mary and Martha. For sisters, Mary and Martha are quite a contrast. Martha, whose name means "mistress," was indeed the mistress or overseer of hospitality in her house. She welcomes (verse 38) Jesus into her home as was fitting and expected (Luke 10:7). She busily turns to the tasks of hospitality and becomes irritated when Mary does not help (verse 40). Her irritation leads to a scolding by Jesus. Martha is upset with Mary and also with her Lord for allowing Mary to sit listening at his feet while she scurries around to prepare for her guest. Jesus says Martha is "distracted." This means "to be pulled or dragged away" (verse 41). Martha may have wished to listen to Jesus, too, but the many household tasks she has *drag* her away from him. Jesus also calls Martha "worried." This means "being anxious or unduly concerned."

> **To express hospitality** in Jesus' time, it was customary for people to wash and care for the feet of their guests when they removed their sandals as they entered the home. Mary anointed Jesus' feet with perfume (John 12).

Mary is quite the opposite. She sits "at the Lord's feet" and listens to him (verse 39). This is the customary position of a pupil or disciple before a teacher (Acts 22:3). Mary's position shows her eagerness to learn from Jesus. It is very significant that Jesus does not discourage her. Generally, Jewish teachers of the day were opposed to women taking the position of a disciple. It is Mary who is breaking the mold. Martha is well within the norm to be critical of her sister, but Jesus does not agree. Instead, he describes Mary as the one who had "chosen the better part," or the "best course" (verse 42). Martha may have been preparing many courses of food, but the best course is Jesus himself. Mary has her priorities straight and rightly values her guest for his presence and his message.

Jesus' words to Martha are sensitive and caring. The double address, "Martha, Martha" (verse 41), is evidence of gentleness. Still, they are words with a clear message for Mary, Martha, and Christians of all generations. There is too much in our lives that can distract us or pull us away from our Lord. Household duties, a job, and even well-meant acts of hospitality or charity can so overwhelm us that we do not have time to worship or learn from our Lord. Our priorities get all mixed up and we, like Martha, end up ignoring the very Lord we are seeking to serve.

Lazarus was Mary and Martha's brother. Jesus raised Lazarus from the dead (John 11).

Like Olivia's children, we become so intent on providing material comforts for others that we substitute them for a face-to-face visit and relationship. As Christians, we are called to a life of service in the name of Jesus. But that service needs to be rooted in our worshipful relationship with our Lord.

Mary and Martha lived in the town Bethany, three miles from Jerusalem.

A Savior, a Song and a Star

What are my actual wants—not my whims, but my needs? I want to feel that living has a truly great reason. I want abiding assurance that days are meaningful, that life has a worthy destination, a dependable Guide, and a sure direction. Iw want something to do and an adequate reason for doing it. I want to hear a voice which says things which do not need to be revised.

I want to be true. I want to be honest. I want to be consistent. I want to be able to pray "thy kingdom come" and "thy will be done" without feeling that I am but a kneeling lie. I want to live with my conscience as I read my Bible.

I want my children to be safe. I want to be happy. I want to be healthy.

I need Christ. Without him there is no significance in my present task and no anchor for my future trial. Without him I choke on every prayer and lift my eyes to a vacant sky.

I want a song, a song that is inspired by an event, that makes an eternal difference, a song that is true. I want this song to sing, but I also want it to give.

Lord, I can never compose this song. Give me a song, I pray.

And then, dear Lord, I want a star to follow, something to look up to.

A savior, a song, and a star—these are my vital needs, and this is my prayer.

Focus the Stories

Update It

Put the story of Mary and Gabriel into a current setting. What town would be Nazareth? What role would Mary have in the community?

Martha and Mary Moments

Where and when do you feel like Martha? What distracts you from worship and learning? Where and when do you feel like Mary? What is meaningful for you about worship and learning?

Mary's Example

In his explanation to the First Commandment, Martin Luther writes, "We are to fear, love, and trust God above all things" (From *A Contemporary Translation of Luther's Small Catechism: Study Edition,* copyright © 1994 Augsburg Fortress). How did Mary the mother of Jesus do this? What could have been her reasons for resisting God's call?

What Do We Do?

Look at your congregation's newsletter, annual report, or worship bulletin. Circle activities of service and put rectangles around activities of worship and learning. How many of each kind of activities are there? Which do you attend? What would you change about the programs offered by your congregation and why?

Is It True?

Have you ever heard anyone say, "Christians are so heavenly minded that they are no earthly good"? Do you agree or disagree? Why?

A Cloud of Witnesses

We are surrounded in the Bible and in our daily lives with many faithful witnesses to the love and faithfulness of God. These people nurture our faith. How would you complete these sentences?

• If I could adopt one characteristic of **Mary the mother of Jesus** it would be _____ because _____.

• If I could adopt one characteristic of **Mary the sister of Martha** it would be _____ because _____.

Closing

With the Lord begin your task;
Jesus will direct it.
For his aid and counsel ask;
Jesus will perfect it.
Ev'ry morn with Jesus rise,
And, when day is ended,
In his name then close your eyes;
Be to him commended.

Text copyright © 1941 Concordia Publishing House. Used by permission.

⑤ Surprising Changes

Jesus Christ brings surprising changes to people's lives.

Matthew 16:13-23 Peter's Confession

Like a Rock

THE BIBLE TELLS US A LOT ABOUT PETER, Jesus' disciple. One moment Peter could be self-confident and strong, and then the next moment he could be fearful and hesitant. We see this early in his travels with Jesus as he attempts to walk on water and nearly drowns (14:28-33). Later, he swears he will never desert Jesus (26:33), only to deny him three times. And it is Peter who impulsively takes up the sword to defend Jesus, only to be scolded and told to put that thing away (John 18:11). No wonder Jesus calls him Peter, the rock. A rock can be very strong and solid, but it can also get in the way.

> **Disciple means** "learner" or "pupil."

Peter, the rock, makes a great confession of faith when he proclaims that Jesus is God's Son (verse 16). This kind of faith is the foundation of God's new community of believers. Peter's confession is a very important turning point in the Gospels of Matthew, Mark, and Luke. It clarifies who Jesus is, and it lays the foundation for what is to follow. The call to discipleship (verses 24-26) and

Mushroom rock near King Solomon's copper mines in the Negev Desert.

Jesus' own suffering (verse 21) are based on this truth: Jesus is the divine Son of God. If we wish to understand Jesus, his ministry, and his death and resurrection, we must grasp what Peter confesses. It is God, present in Jesus, who has come to teach, to forgive, and finally to die and rise for us (3:17; 11:27). Jesus recognizes that Peter has been blessed with faith in order to have answered so well. He knows that "flesh and blood"—that is, human beings—have not revealed this, but rather God.

Jesus names Peter the keeper of the "keys of the kingdom of heaven" (verse 19). The power "to bind" (literally "to forbid") and "to loose" (literally "to permit") in the matters of the assembly of the believers is given to him. This refers primarily to Peter having authority to teach, but also to discipline. Peter can declare a commandment binding or not and can discipline those who break one. Not long after this, similar authority is given to all the disciples (18:18). Jesus is preparing his followers for the future. Peter and the disciples will help provide a foundation, a stability for the assembly of believers after Jesus' departure.

Peter is also a stumbling block. He will not hear of it when Jesus predicts his suffering, death, and resurrection (verses 21-22). His words "God forbid it, Lord! This must never happen to you" (verse 22) show that he cannot comprehend how the very Son of God could be at the mercy of mere human beings and die at their hands. Jesus rebukes him severely

> **Peter and his brother,** Andrew, were fishermen. They lived in Capernaum on the shore of the Sea of Galilee.

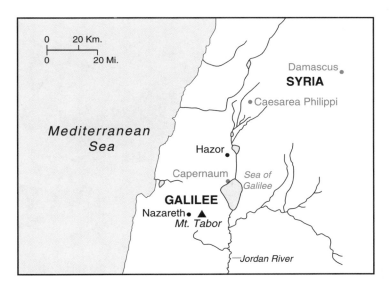

(verse 23). Peter has become a stumbling block because he thinks of only victory and glory and understands nothing of the way of suffering. Jesus uses the strong term *Satan* because Peter, like Satan in the wilderness (4:1-11), is tempting Jesus to take the easy way out and avoid suffering.

If God is to save us from the power of sin and death, it must involve Jesus' suffering, death, and resurrection. There is no other route. Those who will teach and lead in the church must be very clear about this. After Jesus' resurrection (John 21:15-19), Jesus would commission Peter to such a life of service and suffering.

> **Peter may** have been crucified in about A.D. 64.

Acts 9:1-22 Paul's Conversion

Complete Turn Around

THE STORY OF PAUL is a wonderful example of the transforming power of Jesus. Known as Saul, he approaches Damascus something like a fire-breathing dragon (verse 1), persecuting all followers of Jesus. He leaves Damascus soon after this as a preacher and defender of Jesus Christ. It is a complete about-face, which astounds everyone on all sides (verses 13, 21). And it all happens by the grace of God.

Saul had a strict upbringing and traditional Jewish training in the synagogue school at Tarsus. By about age 30, he was a great defender of Judaism and participated whole-heartedly in the persecution of Christians. It was he who witnessed and approved the stoning to death of Stephen (8:1). This persecution began in Jerusalem, and many Christians escaped to other cities like Damascus (8:2). The high priest at Jerusalem commissioned Saul to travel north to arrest any followers of Jesus (9:2). His anger, hatred, and zeal make Saul the perfect man for this "search and destroy mission."

Suddenly, the fire-breathing dragon is laid low (verses 3-4). It is the Lord Jesus who halts Saul in his tracks and turns him from persecutor to confessor. Jesus' words are amazingly gentle, considering all the evil Saul has done. The double address of Saul's name is evidence of this, and it is followed by a question, *not* a condemna-

> **The name *Paul* means** "little."

Saul (Paul) was a member of the tribe of Benjamin.

tion (verse 4). Many Christians at that time would have been elated to hear that Saul, the murderer, had been struck down and killed on the road. But this is not the Lord's way. It is true that Saul is made blind and helpless, but only so that he could see with new eyes and go in a new direction. The powerful Saul is "led" by others into Damascus where he fasts (a sign of repentance) and waits. What a reversal!

The name *Ananias* means "God has been gracious."

Ananias is a key player in this reversal. He has fled the persecution in Jerusalem and is keeping a very low profile. But when his Lord calls, he answers with a response reminiscent of Mary the mother of Jesus (Luke 1:38). He says, "Here I am, Lord" (9:10). Ananias, like Mary, is a model of faith for this new community of believers.

Still, what an unnerving task! He is to go to Saul, the very man he has been fleeing (verse 13). But Jesus assures him that Saul knows of his coming and that all this is necessary to make Saul an "instrument" in God's mission (verse 15). Reassured, Ananias gains courage and goes. When he finds Saul, he addresses him as "Brother Saul" (verse 17), which shows they now share the same Lord. He heals and baptizes Saul, and Saul joins the fellowship of believers (verse 19).

Straight Street was located in a wealthy part of Damascus.

Saul the persecutor becomes Paul the disciple. The Lord Jesus directs Saul's life and preaching. Saul preaches powerfully to the Jews in the synagogue and will eventually do the same to the Gentiles.

> **A second-century** writer described Paul as bald and bowlegged.

Rather than being a source of suffering, he suffers for the sake of Jesus (verse 16). By the grace of God, the persecutor becomes the witness, and this witness spreads around the known world (28:28).

BOOKS OF THE NEW TESTAMENT ATTRIBUTED TO PAUL

Paul founded many churches in Asia Minor and Greece and carried on extensive correspondence with them. His life and work are detailed in the New Testament book Acts of the Apostles and the following letters.

ROMANS	The Message of Salvation • The Problem of the Jews • Life in Christ
1 CORINTHIANS	Dissension in the Church • The Lord's Supper • Gifts of the Spirit • The Resurrection
2 CORINTHIANS	God's Comfort and Mercy • Ambassadors for Christ • Paul's Suffering
GALATIANS	The Gospel of Christ • Life in Christ
EPHESIANS	The Household of God • Christian Living
PHILIPPIANS	The Mind of Christ
COLOSSIANS	The Supremacy of Christ
1 THESSALONIANS	Chirst's Coming Is at Hand
2 THESSALONIANS	Prayer and Praise
1 TIMOTHY	The Christian Ministry
2 TIMOTHY	The Servant's Duties
TITUS	Stewards of God
PHILEMON	The Runaway Slave

Focus the Stories

Turned Around

Think of a time when the Lord Jesus turned you around and changed the direction of your life. Perhaps there was one time when your faith developed, changed, and became stronger. You may have been deeply influenced by a book, a person, or an experience you had.

Foundation Stones and Stumbling Blocks

Who or what are the "rocks" in your life of faith? Name those things or people who have supported you in your faith. Name those "rocks" that stand as obstacles to your faith—things that weaken your faith or tempt you away from worshiping and serving the Lord Jesus.

Public Profession

Peter and Paul are models of faith for us in their confession that Jesus Christ is God's Son our Lord. How and when do we, as the church and individuals, openly confess Jesus as Lord? Why is this sometimes difficult? How could we help one another witness more openly to Jesus Christ as our Lord?

No Pain, No Gain

The above phrase is often used in reference to physical exercise. Could it fit the life of faith? How? Does it fit the lives of Paul, Peter, Ananias, and Jesus? How about your life?

A Cloud of Witnesses

We are surrounded in the Bible and in our daily lives with many faithful witnesses to the love and faithfulness of God. These people nurture our faith. How would you complete these sentences?

- If I could adopt one characteristic of **Peter** it would be _____ because _____.
- If I could adopt one characteristic of **Paul** it would be _____ because _____.

Closing

Lord of all, of Church and kingdom,
in an age of change and doubt
keep us faithful to the Gospel;
help us work your purpose out.
Here, in this day's dedication,
all we have to give, receive;
we, who cannot live without you,
we adore you! We believe!